Original title:
The Frozen Earth Sings

Copyright © 2024 Creative Arts Management OÜ
All rights reserved.

Author: Colin Leclair
ISBN HARDBACK: 978-9916-94-532-2
ISBN PAPERBACK: 978-9916-94-533-9

Chilling Notes of the Silent Night

In winter's grip, the snowflakes dance,
They twirl and spin, not missing a chance.
With frosty breaths, they clap and cheer,
A chilly concert, the best of the year.

The penguins waddle, a merry band,
With tiny top hats, looking quite grand.
They sing their tunes in a winter trance,
While polar bears join, not missing the chance.

Resonance of the Icy Shadows

Icy shadows creep and slide,
With snowmen laughing, taking pride.
They toss snowballs like a pro,
In this frosty, funny show.

The icicles chime, a glimmering tune,
Under the watch of a chuckling moon.
They wink at rabbits, fluffy and fast,
As they hop past, their snowballs cast.

The Crystal Choir at Dusk

Beneath the stars, the crystals gleam,
A choir of frost, a whimsical dream.
With snowflakes giggling, in sync they sing,
Laughter echoes, a magical thing.

The winter critters, all in a line,
Dress up for the show, looking divine.
With a tap of paws on the ice so slick,
The concert begins, and it's quite the kick!

Resonance of the Icy Shadows

Icy shadows creep and slide,
With snowmen laughing, taking pride.
They toss snowballs like a pro,
In this frosty, funny show.

The icicles chime, a glimmering tune,
Under the watch of a chuckling moon.
They wink at rabbits, fluffy and fast,
As they hop past, their snowballs cast.

The Crystal Choir at Dusk

Beneath the stars, the crystals gleam,
A choir of frost, a whimsical dream.
With snowflakes giggling, in sync they sing,
Laughter echoes, a magical thing.

The winter critters, all in a line,
Dress up for the show, looking divine.
With a tap of paws on the ice so slick,
The concert begins, and it's quite the kick!

Echoing Frost: A Winter's Ode

In the frosty morn, the world's a stage,
With squirrels chattering, they engage.
The trees wear coats, all sparkly and bright,
As they join in the quirky, winter plight.

Their whispers fly on the chilly breeze,
Tickling noses and toes with ease.
While snowflakes giggle, they tumble and glide,
In this freezing fun, let joy be our guide.

Glittering Silence of the Frozen World

In winter's grip, a snowman glows,
With carrot nose and funny toes.
His friends all laugh, they can't believe,
A snowman with a dance to weave.

Icicles hang down like giant spears,
While polar bears shed friendly tears.
They slip and slide on icy slopes,
And play like kids with silly hopes.

The trees wear coats of frosty white,
As squirrels prance in pure delight.
They hide their acorns, go for a spin,
And chase their tails, their laughter thin.

So here we are, the world aglow,
With whirling flakes in a joyful show.
Let's toast to winter, let's all be merry,
Where echoes of giggles are never scary.

Winter's Timeless Rhythms

Chilly air plays a tune so sweet,
As penguins waddle on clumsy feet.
They slide and tip, a comedy scene,
In their tuxedos, they reign supreme!

Frosty windows hide giggles inside,
While cocoa cups take winter's ride.
Laughter bubbles like hot chocolate,
In every mug, let's celebrate it!

Snowflakes dance like sprightly jesters,
As children build their frosty testers.
A snowball flies, then all retreat,
In this snowy game, they can't be beat!

The moon looks down with a knowing grin,
As winter's laughter begins to spin.
With joy we rally, this chill we tarry,
In rhythms of fun, we'll always be merry.

Notes of a Snowy Reverie

In quiet woods, the snowflakes fall,
They tickle noses, surprise us all.
A deer looks up with a puzzled stare,
Wondering why it's wearing air!

With snowmen grinning, mischief brews,
They plan a laugh without a clue.
A hat askew, a scarf askance,
Join in their wobbly winter dance!

The winds whisper jokes in frosty breath,
While geese play cards, not fearing death.
They cackle loud, their feathers fluff,
Winter's a stage—enough is enough!

So gather 'round, let joy unfold,
In this snowy realm where dreams are bold.
With giggles galore, let's make it clear,
That laughter in winter is always near.

Songs Carved in the Snow

Snowflakes dance in the bright moonlight,
Rabbits hop and try to take flight.
A snowman strums on a carrot nose,
While the winter wind humorously blows.

Penguins waddle in their tight little suits,
Singing bass lines while shaking their boots.
Icicles jingle like chimes in a breeze,
Nature's comic show brings us to our knees.

Icy Harmonies of the Night Sky

Stars above want to join in the jest,
Twinkling bright, they think they're the best.
The moon chuckles at clouds floating by,
As they puff up like marshmallows high.

A comet bursts into giggles and cheer,
While frosty critters lend their ear.
With a wink from the frost, the night carries on,
Setting the stage till the daylight is gone.

Nature's Lullaby in White

Under the blanket of soft swirling snow,
A teddy bear whispers secrets to frogs below.
Squirrels play tag amongst branches above,
While snowflakes flutter like hearts full of love.

The trees shake their limbs in a dance so obscure,
They giggle as nature's little creatures endure.
Hilarious how snowmen can't seem to stand,
But their carrot noses come up with a plan.

The Cold's Serene Chorus

Huddled together, the geese take a vote,
On which of them sings best with a coat.
A chorus of chuckles fills icy blue air,
As they flap and squawk without any care.

Frosty flakes whisper old jokes from the past,
While the humor of winter seems to hold fast.
With snow as the stage, they laugh 'til they tire,
Nature's comedy leaves us all to admire.

Chill's Embrace: A Melodic Tale

In winter's grasp, all critters freeze,
Chattering teeth 'neath icy trees.
A penguin slips, with quite the flair,
Waddling home, without a care.

Snowballs fly from squirrels high,
A frosty chill, a laugh, a sigh.
The rabbits dance, they can't be beat,
Toes are footloose, on frosty feet.

A snowman winks, with carrot nose,
"Hey there, friend! Do you like my pose?"
A shiver runs through all the trees,
As branches shake with winter's tease.

Hushed Harmony Under Ice

A seal plays chess with a sleepy bear,
"Checkmate!" he yells, without a care.
Snowflakes fall, a white confetti,
As penguins laugh, all warm and sweaty.

The icicles drip, a musical beat,
Tap dancing penguins, oh so sweet!
Frosty hiccups from the snowmen's grins,
In winter's world, the fun begins!

Sledding squirrels zoom down the hill,
Landing in snow with quite the thrill.
"A little help?" they call with glee,
As snowballs fly, "Come play with me!"

An Arctic Elegy

A polar bear with a fuzzy hat,
Sips cocoa while he chats with a cat.
"Is it cold?" the feline asks, aglow,
"Just chilly enough to steal the show!"

From crackling ice, they hear a cheer,
"Let's start a snowball fight, my dear!"
With every toss, laughter shakes the ground,
As winter's wonderland spins around.

A walrus hums a jolly tune,
While igloos dance beneath the moon.
"Who knew cold could feel so warm?"
With jokes and jests, the season's charm.

Rhythms of the Winter's Edge

In frosty lands, the fun takes flight,
Snowflakes twirl, all day and night.
A moose attempts ballet with grace,
Tripping o'er ice, a comical face.

The owls chuckle from their lofty perch,
As animals gather for a winter search.
"Who has the best freeze?" they playfully ask,
With poses that could be quite the task.

In snowy woods, the laughter spreads,
As cuddly creatures bounce in their beds.
The chill might bite, but oh what fun,
In this frosty land, we've just begun!

Ballads of the Bitter Cold

In the winter's chill, the penguins dance,
Waddling around, they take a chance.
Snowflakes giggle as they fall down low,
Skating on ice, 'they're quite the show.'

The squirrels are sneezing in their warm nests,
Their winter coats at their furry behests.
Hot cocoa spills as they run to play,
Happy in snow, come what may.

Resonance of Crystal Dreams

Frosty windows with doodles and glee,
Cats in pajamas, as cozy as can be.
The icicles chime like a ridiculous bell,
Annoying the dogs, they bark quite as well.

Snowmen gossip with carrot-nose flair,
Whispering secrets flying through the air.
With hats askew, they argue with pride,
Over who gets the best frosty slide.

Frosted Verses in the Twilight

In the faerie lights, the snowflakes twirl,
Dancing like they've had too much whirl.
A snowball fight breaks in laughter and screams,
Turns to ice cream dreams, or so it seems.

The moon beams down with a shimmering grin,
Winking at bunnies, drawing them in.
With snow for dessert, they start to munch,
Their fluffy cheeks full, oh what a bunch!

Balladry of the Icy Landscape

The cold winds whistle a funny old tune,
While bears in pajamas sleep under the moon.
They dream of donuts, warm and round,
Unknowing that frost is all that is found.

Old trees creak as they stretch to yawn,
Talking to owls with a nervous fawn.
With each frozen branch like a tickled foot,
Winter's humor, oh how cute!

Whispers of Winter's Heart

Beneath the snow, a squirrel schemes,
Wearing a hat of frosty dreams.
He plans a dance on ice so slick,
But ends up slipping – what a trick!

The penguins gather, all in a line,
With shades and flip-flops, looking divine.
They waddle and slide, a comical sight,
Who knew they'd party in the moonlight?

A snowman grins, with carrot nose,
And tells cool jokes, everyone knows.
He claims that snowball fights are fair,
But loses his head when tossed in the air!

So laugh with me 'neath the chilly skies,
With snowflakes diving, oh how they fly!
In winter's chill, there's warmth in cheer,
As frosty giggles fill the year.

Chords Beneath the Snow

A bunny hops with a ukulele,
In worship of winter, oh so jolly.
He strums a tune while sliding by,
As snowflakes dance, oh me, oh my!

A moose on skates does a pirouette,
Wobbling wildly, oh what a threat!
He tries to sing but goes off-key,
The whole forest chortles, wild with glee.

Icicles hang like a treble clef,
Chilling the breeze, a frozen chef.
They twinkle like stars, oh what a treat,
As frosty musicians play on repeat!

So join the choir, with snowflakes bright,
Winter's concert is pure delight.
Raise your voice, let laughter flow,
In a symphony of ice and snow.

Whispers of Winter's Heart

Beneath the snow, a squirrel schemes,
Wearing a hat of frosty dreams.
He plans a dance on ice so slick,
But ends up slipping – what a trick!

The penguins gather, all in a line,
With shades and flip-flops, looking divine.
They waddle and slide, a comical sight,
Who knew they'd party in the moonlight?

A snowman grins, with carrot nose,
And tells cool jokes, everyone knows.
He claims that snowball fights are fair,
But loses his head when tossed in the air!

So laugh with me 'neath the chilly skies,
With snowflakes diving, oh how they fly!
In winter's chill, there's warmth in cheer,
As frosty giggles fill the year.

Chords Beneath the Snow

A bunny hops with a ukulele,
In worship of winter, oh so jolly.
He strums a tune while sliding by,
As snowflakes dance, oh me, oh my!

A moose on skates does a pirouette,
Wobbling wildly, oh what a threat!
He tries to sing but goes off-key,
The whole forest chortles, wild with glee.

Icicles hang like a treble clef,
Chilling the breeze, a frozen chef.
They twinkle like stars, oh what a treat,
As frosty musicians play on repeat!

So join the choir, with snowflakes bright,
Winter's concert is pure delight.
Raise your voice, let laughter flow,
In a symphony of ice and snow.

Echoes of Icebound Souls

A polar bear in a fluffy hat,
Dances about, how about that?
He juggles fish, what a sight,
Till one slips away in pure delight!

Frogs in mittens croak a tune,
Singing love songs 'neath a chilly moon.
With frosty breath, they serenade,
Hoping for warmth through their escapade.

Snowballs fly, a playful fight,
Chasing shadows into the night.
With every throw, a laugh goes up,
In this frozen world, we fill the cup.

So grab your friends, let the fun unfold,
In icy laughter, let stories be told.
For winter's chill can tickle the soul,
Making frosty hearts feel wonderfully whole.

Melodies in the Glacial Wind

A crow in shades croons to the snow,
While icy gusts lend a frosty blow.
He styles his feathers, oh so brash,
With every note, he makes a splash!

Two trees gossip with branches wide,
About the cold and their furry ride.
They laugh of whispers that winter brings,
As pinecones fall like hidden swings.

A fox in boots leaps with a shout,
Dodging snowdrifts with a playful flout.
In a twist and twirl, he finds his groove,
In this winter wonder, he makes a move!

So let's disgrace the winter chill,
With laughter loud and snowy thrill.
For in this spectacle of icy whim,
The melodies of joy forever brim.

Tapestry of Ice and Light

Beneath the cold and glimmering sky,
Penguins waddle, looking quite spry.
Snowmen giggle, they can't deny,
Holding snowballs, they lift up high.

Icicles dangle like frozen teeth,
Bears slip and slide, oh what a feat!
Ice cream dreams on a frosty street,
Chilly laughter, a wintery treat!

Snowflakes dance in a flurry of glee,
Making wishes as they swirl with spree.
The chill can't stop such jolly spree,
Nature's humor is truly the key.

A snowball fight with a frosty twist,
Each throw accompanied by a frosty mist.
In this winter wonder, who could resist?
Life in the cold is much too blissed!

Chants of the Subzero Night

Under the blanket of sparkling frost,
Icicles shimmer, never quite lost.
Elks tell jokes of what they've crossed,
Such laughter echoes, a merry cost.

Chilling winds hum through pine and oak,
Sleds go zipping with a laugh, a joke.
Frosty whispers from every yoke,
As if winter's a spirited bloke.

Stars twinkle bright with a cheeky grin,
Snowflakes tumble, oh where to begin?
Crisp frosty air, let's take it in,
In each moment, joy is bound to win.

Under the moon in a powdery white,
Snowflakes prance in the pale moonlight.
The cold may bite, but oh, what a sight!
Subzero fun makes the heart feel light!

Dreaming in a Still White Place

In this dream where snowflakes swirl,
Polar bears dance and penguins twirl.
Snowmen wear hats, giving a whirl,
In a winter's tale, oh what a pearl!

Silence blankets the world so wide,
Whispers of laughter in snowflakes glide.
Bunny hops with a frosty stride,
Chasing his shadow, he's filled with pride.

Ducks wearing scarves, what a delight!
Sliding around on a frozen kite.
In crisp white, hearts feel so light,
Joyful moments, a lovely sight!

Frosty dreams hang like breath in the air,
A snowball fight is a snowy affair.
Here in this stillness, let's take a dare,
To find joy in winter, beyond compare!

Frosty Murmurs of the Forgotten

Whispers of frost in the quiet night,
Shadows dance in the pale moonlight.
Old trees chuckle, holding on tight,
As the world around them takes flight.

The snowflakes tell tales, soft and sweet,
Of silly critters with frosty feet.
Laughter echoes on this wintry street,
Where every moment feels like a treat.

In the chilly embrace, memories play,
Snowball warriors in a grand display.
Frozen giggles in a light-hearted fray,
Winter's humor is here to stay!

Lost in a shiver, we find our cheer,
Bundled in layers, we persevere.
With frost-kissed smiles that feel oh so dear,
In winter's arms, there's nothing to fear!

Hymn of the Winter's Breath

Snowflakes dance on chilly air,
Like wiggly worms without a care.
They tumble down with joyful squeaks,
Playing hide and seek for weeks.

Trees wear coats of icy lace,
As squirrels gather for a race.
They chatter loudly, what a sight!
In this frosty, funny flight.

Frosty breath like dragons puff,
Making chilly contests tough.
Hot cocoa dreams and laughter loud,
We're the silliest winter crowd.

So let's embrace this wintry spree,
With snowball fights and hot green tea.
Our breath turns clouds in frosty sun,
In this wacky world, we're all just fun.

Notes from the Crystal Canopy

Icicles hang like crystal chimes,
Singing silly winter rhymes.
The snowmen grin with carrot nose,
And share the secrets nobody knows.

Penguins skate with craft and glee,
In a frosty ballet, can't you see?
They slip and slide, a comic show,
In the chilly, giggly glow.

Frosted windows, misty art,
Draw funny faces that melt the heart.
Each chilly breeze a playful tease,
Brr! Who knew winter could please?

Chasing snowflakes, we all play,
In a winter wonderland ballet.
With laughter loud, the world feels bright,
In this chilly land, we take flight.

Whispers of Winter's Breath

Whispers float on winter's breeze,
Tickling cheeks like little tease.
Snowflakes whisper, 'Catch me quick!'
In this frosty, playful trick.

The rabbits bounce on snowy mounds,
Making silly hops and sounds.
With puffy tails and joyful naps,
They dream of carrots and funny laps.

Winter's chill tries to be tough,
But we wear mittens, that's enough.
We slide and glide on frozen lakes,
And giggle at our snowy quakes.

Fireplaces crackle, shadows dance,
As we sip cocoa at a chance.
Each sip a giggle, every sip fun,
In this chilly world, we've nearly won!

Melodies of Ice and Snow

Icebergs dress in white attire,
Swaying gently, oh, they inspire!
Frosty hats and silly gloves,
Winter laughs as all it loves.

Skiers tumble, laughter loud,
Spreading fun, a jovial crowd.
Snowball battles with no real aim,
In this wild, wintry game.

Frosty noses poking through,
Funny faces, how about you?
We dance with snowflakes, up and down,
Turning frowns into a crown.

The world glistens, sparkles bright,
As we twirl in the chilly light.
Joy in every frosty note,
As winter's fun we gladly tote.

Frost-Kissed Harmonies

Snowflakes dance on noses, bright,
As penguins wear their ties just right.
The trees all wear a frosty grin,
While squirrels plan their winter spin.

The ice could sing a silly song,
About the days that feel so long.
With hot cocoa spills and playful shouts,
We warm our hearts while snow flurries pout.

The chilly winds let out a sigh,
While frosty beans on toasting fly.
Each breath a cloud, a giggle shared,
In winter's laugh, we find we're dared.

The icicles play harp to the frost,
While snowmen guard the fun that's lost.
In joyful tunes the season hums,
With turtlenecks and winter drums.

Whispers in the Chill

Listen close to frosty fun,
As snowflakes fall and rivers run.
A penguin slips, a cat might freeze,
While winter's whispers tickle trees.

The moon adorns the chilly night,
While owls hoot in comical fright.
Each creature wraps in scarves so bright,
As hot chocolate warms the winter bite.

Skiers fall like bowling pins,
While laughter reigns and joy begins.
A snowball fight breaks out in glee,
As everyone shouts, 'Catch me, catch me!'

The air is crisp with frosty zest,
In woolly hats, we all look best.
Together we create a cheer,
In winter's whirl, we have no fear.

The Slumbering Land's Tune

Under blankets, snuggled tight,
The land is dreaming, oh what a sight!
Pillows piled, the world feels light,
While snowflakes giggle through the night.

The rabbits frolic, dressed in white,
As winter's whispers take the flight.
With tiny feet and chilly breath,
They plot their mischief, with glee and depth.

The trees are snoozing, wrapped in a quilt,
While icicles dance, with nimble tilt.
A snowman snores, his carrot hat,
In slumber's grip, the world's a brat.

When morning breaks with cheesy rays,
And frost melts into playful plays.
All are stirred from dreams so sweet,
In winter's wonder, we find our beat.

Breath of the Winter Moon

When the moon beams down the icy glow,
The world ignites with fun, you know.
Snowflakes giggle, as they fall,
Twirling, whirling, having a ball.

The squirrels gather for a feast,
While chipmunks plan their prankish tease.
Mittens lost in snowdrift piles,
Chasing winter's tricks with silly smiles.

Each star twinkles, a frosty tease,
As winter sways with graceful ease.
The breeze is filled with giggles bright,
In moonlit shadows of the night.

We toast with cocoa, hearts aglow,
In the frosty air, let laughter flow.
With cheeks aglow and spirits high,
While winter dances beneath the sky.

Winter's Gentle Cadence

Snowflakes dance and twirl around,
A frosty jester on the ground.
They stick like glue to your warm nose,
Tickling toes in winter's clothes.

Icicles hang like frozen spears,
With each drip, releasing cheers.
Sleds flying by, laughter in the air,
A snowball fight turns into a scare!

Hot cocoa waits with marshmallow cheer,
As penguins wobble, drawing near.
Snowmen wear hats like funky kings,
In this chilly world, joy springs.

So grab your scarf and join the fun,
Let's play until the day is done.
Winter's tune is a cheeky grin,
In this frosty land, we all win!

Shards of Melody in the Cold

A frozen tune plays in the park,
Where snowmen dance until it's dark.
With carrot noses joined in glee,
They shake and shimmy, wild and free.

Ice crystals jingle like silly bells,
While rabbits hop and cast their spells.
The squirrels wear tiny earmuffs bright,
Hosting a rave under the moonlight.

Laughter echoes in snowy halls,
Where penguins slide and take big falls.
A snowflake chorus sings out loud,
Drawing in every giggly crowd.

Everything sparkles, a glittery spree,
Join in the fun, it's all free!
In every flake, a joke so bold,
In this winter realm, warmth takes hold!

A Symphony of Snowflakes

In winter's hall, the tunes do play,
As snowflakes swirl in their ballet.
Dancing down like little queens,
They tickle noses and fill the scenes.

Frosty air brings a slapstick glow,
As children tumble in the snow.
Snowball bombs and giggles galore,
Winter antics we can't ignore.

The wind whistles a playful song,
With every gust, we can't go wrong.
With mittens on, we clap our hands,
Creating laughter across the lands.

So slide and glide, take to the slopes,
In this frosty realm, we weave our hopes.
Every flake a note, together they play,
In winter's symphony, we find our way!

Dreams in a White Enchantment

In a blanket of white, dreams unfold,
As children giggle, shivering cold.
Snowball fights turn into fashion shows,
Decked out in layers from head to toes.

A wintry world, a canvas so pure,
With snowmen that wobble and unsure.
They wave their arms, greet every face,
In this frosty wonderland, what a place!

Fluffy clouds bring a soft embrace,
While sleds rocket down, in joyful race.
Cocoa spills with laughter's burst,
In this brisk land, we quench our thirst.

So make a wish on a snowy night,
With giggles and glee, everything feels right.
Dreams of snowflakes, icy delight,
In laughter and joy, our hearts ignite!

Strings of Icebound Time

In cold halls where giggles freeze,
Icicles play tunes in the breeze.
Snowmen wear hats that are far too grand,
And snowflakes dance like a marching band.

Chilly whispers choke on their laughs,
As winter jokes get printed on staffs.
Frosty winds tickle the trees,
And squirrels dart by with a squeal of ease.

Icicles drip in a sticky retort,
As the sun teases with a warm support.
Crystals twinkle like sequins bright,
Taking snaps in the gleaming light.

Days are bright, but nights are absurd,
With penguins in tuxes looking disturbed.
In this realm of ice, there's no crime,
Just laughter, love, and vibes sublime.

The Symphony of Snowdrifts

Softly the snow falls with an aim,
As flakes compete in a wacky game.
Each one a note in a frosty score,
Dancing and swirling, and begging for more.

Rabbit bands play on, unaware,
That their carrot-flute's lost somewhere.
The owls hoot laughs from their cozy lair,
While snowflakes tickle the winter air.

Mountains giggle beneath their white coats,
While yetis rock out on invisible boats.
Icebergs shuffle on the frosty sea,
Winking at seals, all jolly and free.

A blanket of snow covers the ground,
While cool breezes hum a tuneful sound.
The chill brings giggles, a joyful sight,
In this symphony, all feels just right.

Silhouettes in a Frosty Muse

Shadows play tricks on crisp, clear nights,
A yeti in shades throws zany sights.
With snowball fights, the moon can't resist,
As laughter erupts in the frosty mist.

The penguins glide with flippered flair,
Waddling proud, without a care.
A fox does ballet right near the stream,
In frosty costumes, they're living the dream.

Snowy sentries guard icy gates,
While snowmen gossip on hilarious fates.
Each shape tells stories of merriment pure,
In this frostbitten realm, laughter's the cure.

As moonbeams sprinkle the melting ground,
Frosty shades jive to the chaos around.
It's a theater of giggles, a shivering muse,
In hugs of cold cheer, they all cannot lose.

Snowflakes' Dance on Silence's Stage

On silky stages, silence is bold,
Where snowflakes audition in sparkles unfold.
Each twirl and twist springs giggles alive,
As winter's mischief begins to revive.

Chattering rabbits take center stage,
With hops and skips that leap from the page.
A snowball flies through the crisp night air,
And hits a fox with a surprised stare.

Under the stars, they swirl and spin,
As laughter erupts; let the fun begin!
Frosty confetti falls from above,
While each little snowflake dances with love.

As whispers of winter tickle the heart,
Our frozen friends play their quirky part.
Winding paths of snow shimmer and gleam,
In the dance of silence, a winter dream.

Midnight's Frosty Waltz

In the moonlight's chilly glow,
Snowflakes dance with quite a show.
A penguin slips, with grace so rare,
And lands right in a snowman's hair.

A snowball flies, but misses wide,
It hits a cat, who runs to hide.
The trees are giggling, branches sway,
As squirrels wear scarves in bright array.

With frosty breath, the night does hum,
While bunnies leap, oh what a thrum!
A laugh erupts from frozen heights,
Winter's jest, in joyful flights.

So join the dance in winter's glow,
Where laughter mingles with the snow.
With every slip and frosty spin,
The cold's a place where fun begins.

Snowbound Sonnet of Solitude

In solitude, I find my cheer,
With frosty friends that appear near.
A snowman winks, his carrot grin,
As if to say, 'Let's all jump in!'

The flakes in spirals, twirl and glide,
While penguins play and leap with pride.
A polar bear in fuzzy socks,
Plays hide and seek behind the rocks.

The ice-capped pond, a mirror bright,
Reflects my dance in pure delight.
A snowshoe hare joins in the race,
While winter's smile warms up the place.

So here I sit, with cup in hand,
As laughter echoes through the land.
In frozen stillness, joy takes flight,
A snowy world, a sweet invite.

Echoes of Frost-Laden Dreams

When dreams take shape in icy glow,
And snowflakes whisper soft and low.
A moose in boots tends to his hat,
While chipmunks toss a silly spat.

The frosty air, a playful breeze,
Uplifted spirits, full of ease.
A sled dog snores, his dreams quite grand,
Of chasing tails across the land.

The stars above, with twinkling flair,
Seem to wink down from their lair.
As frosty figures build a maze,
With clumsy moves, we all get praise.

So join the fun, embrace the jest,
In dreams alight with frosty zest.
A world of laughter, cold and bright,
Where every step is pure delight.

Celestial Chimes on Winter Nights

Under stars that twinkle bright,
The snowflakes melt with pure delight.
A polar bear, with socks, he prances,
While frostbit squirrels lead in dances.

The chilly air, a songbird's tune,
As mice march out beneath the moon.
With laughter echoing through the dark,
The winter treats us, leaving a mark.

A rabbit hops in rainbow socks,
While snowmen gossip 'round the rocks.
The sky erupts in snowflake joy,
As winter plays its favorite toy.

So toast to frosty, jolly sights,
Where everything warms on winter nights.
With every tickle of snow's embrace,
Our hearts find laughter in this place.

The Symphony of Silent Flakes

In the air, snowflakes twirl,
Like tiny dancers in a whirl.
They tickle noses, dance past ears,
Making us giggle, stifling cheers.

Each flake unique, a frosty show,
Some are shy, while others glow.
They whisper secrets as they land,
With all their sparkle, never planned.

A snowman laughs with carrot nose,
Wears a scarf made of winter prose.
He tells a joke, the trees all grin,
While bunnies hop, let the joy begin.

When winter's chill claims all the ground,
The giggling winds are the only sound.
So grab your mittens, join the spree,
The frosty fun is waiting, whee!

Rhythms of the Chilled Sky

Up above, a cloud parade,
Puffy shapes, they're not afraid.
They tease the sun, say 'not today',
While snowflakes laugh in frosted play.

Icicles hang like jagged teeth,
As frosty breezes bring relief.
They whisper jokes to passing birds,
"Why stick to branches? What's the word?"

Snowmen hold their winter meet,
Discussing whose nose is the best treat.
They roll and tumble, causing glee,
While squirrels judge from their lofty tree.

The chilly air, it sparkles bright,
With every breath, a frosty bite.
Laughter echoes, soft and spry,
As snowflakes dance beneath the sky.

Nocturne of the Winter Veil

Underneath the starry quilt,
The world is wrapped in snowy silt.
Nighttime giggles stir the air,
Snowflakes tease with frosty flair.

Foxes prance in silver coats,
With sneaky grins, they tell their notes.
"Look! A snowball! Who will throw?"
And off they dart, a snowy show.

The moonlight glimmers, soft and bold,
On old trees that shiver from the cold.
With every sway, they join the jest,
In this silent night, they dance their best.

So when you wander through the chill,
Listen close; let laughter fill.
For winter's cloak, though crisp and white,
Encourages fun on every night.

Songs of Frostbitten Pines

The pines wear coats of icy lace,
Whispering tunes in this frosty place.
With every gust, they sway and bend,
    Holding secrets like a friend.

Beneath their boughs, a snowball fight,
    Laughter echoes, pure delight.
Squirrels chirp their little rhymes,
In winter's orchestra of chimes.

They mix and mingle, branches dance,
    A jolly sight, as if by chance.
The snowflakes join in, laugh out loud,
Creating joy that's winter proud.

So spin and twirl in winter's song,
And with each laugh, you can't go wrong.
For in this chill, with every grin,
The magic of frost will always win.

The Silence of Snowflakes Dancing

Snowflakes flutter with a twist,
Hats on heads, they dance with bliss.
Down they fall, then start to twirl,
Hiding secrets, they softly swirl.

They tickle noses, tease our cheeks,
Whispering jokes as winter peaks.
Laughter lingers on the ground,
In their frosty world, joy's found.

With sleds of kids in snowball fights,
Causing giggles on chilly nights.
Snowmen grinning from ear to ear,
Holding scarves like they're hoarding cheer.

When winter comes, don't take a frown,
Join the flurry, let's all clown!
In frosty fluff, let's twirl away,
As snowflakes dance and shout hooray!

Ode to the Frozen Dusk

Sunset drapes in ice-cold hues,
Chattering squirrels in little shoes.
Footprints lead where laughter's loud,
In frozen fields, we play so proud.

At dusk, the shadows creep and glide,
Chasing snowflakes that dare to hide.
We build a fort, make snowball round,
Armies clash with giggles unwound.

The chilly breeze gives us a wink,
As we tumble, slip, and think.
"Are we snowmen? Who can tell?
Just here for laughs, we ring the bell!"

So here's to dusk, and all its art,
A canvas of laughter warms the heart.
Beneath the chill, a fire's glow,
In frozen dusk, let our joy flow!

Verses in the Winter's Whisper

In winter's hush, a giggle flies,
As snowballs form from crafty spies.
Whispers weave through frosty trees,
Nature chuckles with a teasing breeze.

Icicles hang like frozen grins,
As winter's music softly spins.
Sleds racing down the glistening lane,
Falling laughter, not a hint of pain.

Beneath the snow, the rabbits hop,
Tripping over, they never stop.
Whiskers twitching, eyes aglow,
In the whimsy of winter's show.

As night descends, the stars are bright,
We huddle close, sharing delight.
In winter's lull, we spin and sway,
Sing soft verses, let fun lead the way!

Chilling Calls of Nature's Heart

The trees wear coats, all frosted fine,
Chilly whispers, like aged wine.
Nature calls with an icy tone,
Let's laugh together, you're not alone.

Little feet in boots that squeak,
Waddle like penguins, oh what a peak!
Snowflakes giggle as they collide,
In a sparkling mess, we all abide.

Nature's heart plays peek-a-boo,
Chilling songs with a twist or two.
From frozen ponds to frosty trails,
Every step gives life funny tales.

So let us frolic, high and free,
In the chill, we're a sight to see.
With snowball fights and laughter bright,
We paint the snow with pure delight!

Serenade of Silent Glaciers

In winter's grip, they waltz and sway,
With icy twirls, they dance all day.
Chained to the ground, no feet to roam,
They giggle softly, calling it home.

Snowflakes chuckle, they tickle the nose,
While frozen rivers tell jokes that glows.
Polar bears practice their stand-up sets,
As seals sip cocoa, sharing their bets.

Icicles dangle, a comedy crew,
With knock-knock jokes, they always construe.
The mountains snicker, the valleys grin,
In a chilly world where the laughter's a win.

So raise a toast with a frosty cheer,
To the icebound jesters we hold so dear.
They may be silent, but oh, what a show,
In the land of white where the chuckles flow.

Echoes Beneath the Frost

Under layers thick, beneath the chill,
Echoes of laughter, they rise up at will.
A snowman debates with a friendly crow,
About who made the best snowball throw.

Bubbles of laughter from frozen streams,
Fish telling tales of their fanciful dreams.
A mammoth's joke gets lost in the snow,
As snowflakes giggle, letting it go.

With every flake, a punchline falls,
Even the squirrels are snorting in halls.
The wise old owl, a comedian grand,
Cracks a wise joke while winging the land.

So come join the fun, don't miss this song,
In the frosty realms where we all belong.
Each freeze-dried chuckle and icy delight,
In echoes beneath, brings laughter to light.

Hymn of the Shivering Pines

Pines dressed in white, shake off the frost,
"Don't blame us, dear friends, for the warmth that we lost!"
The branches all quiver, in giggles they sway,
While the squirrels all laugh at the sun's lost ballet.

With jackets of snow, they strut with glee,
Challenging winter to come have a spree.
"Let's throw a party, with candles of light,
And share weird stories in the shivery night."

The chilly winds whistle a tune in their boughs,
As the pines hold a concert, with applause and bows.
"Who needs summer with all this cool flair?
We'll keep on singing, for we just don't care!"

So join the pines, in their frosty jubilee,
Where laughter and ice blend so perfectly.
In the joys of the cold, we're never alone,
With the shivering pines, our laughter is grown.

Ballad of the Snowbound Valley

In a valley dusted with blankets of white,
The snowmen gather for their annual fight.
They roll and they tumble, tripping for fun,
Stumbling 'round like they've all just begun.

Each flake is a giggle, as light as can be,
Dancing around, setting their spirits free.
While rabbits in boots try to join in the cheer,
Hopping and slipping, it's all quite a sphere.

The snowflakes fall down with a comic flair,
As squirrels in nut hats give winter a scare.
"A freeze-frame moment!" they shout in delight,
With icicles swinging as stars in the night.

While winter locks down, the valley's a stage,
Where laughter erupts, setting free from the cage.
In a snowbound valley, the mirth never ends,
With warm-hearted jokes, where the laughter transcends.

Winter's Crystal Ballad

A snowman slips on icy ground,
His carrot nose flies right around.
Children laugh, they cannot wait,
For hot cocoa and a slice of fate.

Frosty friends in hats so bright,
Slip and slide, what a silly sight.
With snowballs thrown and giggles loud,
Winter's mischief makes us proud.

Now penguins waddle to the scene,
In skates too big, they feel quite lean.
Their flapping wings can't find their flair,
As they tumble through the frosty air.

Yet through the chill, we feel the cheer,
Hot chocolate waiting, oh so near!
In every flake and every chill,
Lies laughter's warmth, a joyful thrill.

Silenced by the Snow

In white pajamas, trees stand still,
But squirrels plot their winter thrill.
One takes a dive, no fear in sight,
Falling through fluff, what a fright!

Frosty whispers in the air,
As penguins dance without a care.
Their flippers fail, they spin around,
In a snowy whirl, they hit the ground.

Snowflakes twirl like tiny jesters,
Playing games as winter's testers.
They land on noses, tongues, and toes,
Making magic where nobody knows.

But oh, the laughter echoes wide,
In a snowball fight, we take our pride.
With cheeks aglow and spirits high,
We share the warmth beneath the sky.

Chilled Verses of the Evergreens

Evergreens stand tall and proud,
Dressed in white, they form a crowd.
But watch for critters at their feet,
A deer in snow boots can't be beat!

A bear in winter's napping spree,
Wakes just to snack on lemon tea.
With honey jars and silly grins,
He stumbles back where trouble begins.

Snowflakes dance upon the breeze,
While rabbits hop, they tease the trees.
Their fluffy tails a comic sight,
As they dart under the moonlight.

In every drift and snowy mound,
Jokes and giggles can be found.
For laughter warms through frosty nights,
In our cozy, chilly delights.

An Ode to Glacial Dreams

On icy ponds where children glide,
With socks on hands, they slip and slide.
A tumble here, a splashy fall,
An echoing giggle, a frosty brawl!

With snowman heads that bob and sway,
Their eyes of coal just want to play.
And when the sun begins to peak,
They melt away with one last squeak.

Chasing snowflakes, they shout with glee,
As snowballs fly, they dodge with glee.
What fun we have in frosty air,
As laughter lingers everywhere.

So wrap us tight in winter's cheer,
With every chuckle, winter dear.
For even in the cold's embrace,
A smile ignites, brightens the place.

Frostbitten Reflections

In a land where penguins moan,
Chattering teeth, oh what a tone!
Snowflakes dance on frosty air,
While sledding squirrels shoot a dare.

Icicles drip like frozen tears,
As snowmen plot to conquer fears.
With carrot noses, they take aim,
But hot cocoa breaks the game.

Under blankets, warm and snug,
Dreaming of a woolly bug.
Chasing shadows on the ground,
In this laughter, joy is found.

Yet in this cold, a joke will thrive,
Like frozen peas that come alive.
Laughter echoes through the frost,
In jolly cheer, no giggle lost.

Murmurs Beneath the Snow

Beneath the snow, the critters talk,
A secret club near an old rock.
"Who stole my nuts?" a squirrel squeaks,
As bunnies hop with giggling peaks.

A hedgehog rolls in frosty glee,
While penguins argue, "It's not me!"
Snowflakes tumble, swirl, and play,
Like a merry band on a snowy day.

Over hot drinks, they share their tales,
Of snowball fights and epic fails.
"I swear my snowman grew a grin,"
"I caught him sneaking in a spin!"

Together they laugh, in chilly cheer,
Yearning for spring, but not just yet, dear.
In these moments, heartbeats quick,
As winter's charm does its magic trick.

The Winter's Enchanted Symphony

The winter winds play a tune,
While dancing lights make us swoon.
A melody of frost and ice,
Where silly snowflakes tumble nice.

Fluffy chairs and snowball fights,
Puppies chase with sheer delight.
A chorus of jingle bells rings,
While frosty air some laughter brings.

The trees wear coats of snowy white,
As squirrels dance under moonlight.
With mischief in every paw,
They chatter softly, "What a draw!"

With cocoa swirls, we toast the night,
Our frosty friends, oh what a sight!
In this winter's wondrous play,
We giggle through the icy spray.

Frosted Tranquility

In the quiet of the frozen gleam,
A rabbit dreams a fluffy dream.
With snowflakes falling all around,
Peaceful whispers make their sound.

An old owl hoots a sleepy tune,
While twinkling stars play hide and swoon.
Underneath the frosty glow,
A sleepy world moves soft and slow.

Pine trees chuckle in the breeze,
"Who wants my needles? Not with ease!"
While icicles form a glistening crown,
They sway to nature's quiet sound.

With laughter wrapped in winter's chill,
Awake we stay, against the thrill.
So take a moment, breathe the cheer,
For frosted joy is always near.

A Nocturne of Ice Crystals

In the chill, a snowman laughs,
His carrot nose a joke that halves.
With sticks for arms, they dance around,
While snowflakes swirl without a sound.

The penguins slide with such delight,
Wearing scarves, what a funny sight!
They waddle, tumble in a show,
As icy breezes start to blow.

A polar bear in shades so bright,
Tries to catch an ice fish in flight.
But slips and flips, falls down the hole,
Giggling fishes steal the role.

As frost decorates the tall pine trees,
Squirrels wear hats with playful ease.
Winter's mischief fills the night,
With icy chuckles, pure delight.

Frosty Verses from the Silent Night

A snowflake fashion show is planned,
With frosty couture, all quite grand.
They twirl on air, a dazzling spree,
Laughing till dawn, as free as can be.

The owls wear glasses, wise and bright,
Hosting a party by pale moonlight.
They hoot and holler, what a scene,
While mice in bow ties munch on beans.

A deer in boots, claims he's the king,
But slips and lands in a snowdrift fling.
The moose all cheer, with hearty laughs,
As winter's silliness truly crafts.

With candy canes hung on icy trees,
Elves ride the winds, with endless glee.
Each twinkle and glimmer brings a smile,
As frosty fun spreads for a while.

The Hushed Ballad of Glacial Realms

In a land where ice and giggles meet,
Snowball fights break out in the street.
The snowmen cheer, with hats askew,
While the rabbits join in, quite a crew.

A frost-covered cat in boots so tall,
Struts like a star, proud and small.
Chasing a shadow, he leaps in glee,
For winter's charm is wild and free.

The ice cubes toss in the punch bowl bright,
Making cocktails that spark with light.
As frost fairies dance and take a bow,
While gingerbread men sing, "Carrot now!"

With a tickle of chill and a wink so sly,
Snowflakes fall down, a sprightly pie.
In this frozen world, laughter lingers,
With playful tunes lifted on fingers.

Whispering Pines in Winter's Grasp

Under pines, a party unfolds,
With chattering critters and stories told.
A fox in a tutu leaps with grace,
While the bears groove to an icy bass.

Chirping birds in sweaters bright,
Recite their jokes in morning light.
The world is packed with joyous fun,
Laughter drifting, one by one.

Sliding down hills, the friends collide,
Creating laughter, a winter ride.
The snow gears up for a windy flight,
As snowmen dream through the frostbit night.

With every flake, a giggle appears,
Banishing sorrows and winter fears.
In this snowy realm, let spirits rise,
Where joy reigns bright under wintry skies.

Frosted Threads of Memory

On brisk mornings, socks on the cat,
They march like soldiers, with a tip-tap pat.
Snowflakes tumble, like dancers in glee,
Wishing they'd land on the hot cup of tea.

Old boots lie frozen, stuck in the door,
Whispers of warmth, yet they beg for more.
Chasing the ice-cream truck down the lane,
Only to slip like a clown on a train.

The snowman grins, with a carrot for nose,
Sharing his secrets, in frozen prose.
Making snowballs, with viral delight,
While eggnog warms up in the kitchen, just right.

Giggles arise as we plummet on slopes,
With sleds full of dreams and marshmallow hopes.
Catch me if you can, says the white frosty wind,
In this merry ballet, where laughter begins.

The Lament of the Cold Earth

Oh chilly ground, why'd you hide that bowl?
The soup's gone frostbitten, say 'Hello' to coal!
Mittens missing, in a flurry of flight,
As the cat finds a sunbeam to bask in the light.

Puddles turn tricky, like muddy old shoes,
Dancing with shadows, we jump and we cruise.
Ice cream for breakfast, who knew it was bold?
While snowflakes giggle, 'We're just puppies cold!'

Giant icicles dangle like frozen old spears,
The mailman slips by, his life in arrears.
We warn of the dangers, but laughter prevails,
As frost-coated friends swap their humorous tales.

Rolling in snow, 'til we're lumps on the hill,
Sipping shivery cocoa, a warm winter thrill.
Why walk in a straight line, when wiggles are fun?
In this comedy act, we're all star-studded, done!

Silent Etudes Beneath the Snow

Quiet the world, as the flakes do their dance,
While squirrels in mittens plot their next chance.
Frogs hidden away, under blankets of white,
Working on melodies of frosty moonlight.

Chilly chortles emerge from the trees,
As owls wear top hats, and dance in the breeze.
The wind plays a tune, off-key and so bold,
While melting drops giggle, as stories unfold.

Under the surface, where frost gently lays,
Fish toss snowballs, in rippling bays.
Nature's a jester, a whimsical sight,
With ice as confetti, painting the night.

While snowmen audition for Broadway's next show,
With carrots for cues, they steal the frosty glow.
A soft serenade from a winter's old heart,
Where silence can whisper, yet laughs play their part.

Frosty Visions and Vocal Verses

Beware of the shadow that quacks like a duck,
It's just an old snowman, with questionable luck.
Sirens in the snow, oh how they do wail,
Floating on sleds like a ship's merry sail.

Snowflakes argue about who's first to land,
A contest of patience, uncoordinated band.
With snowball precision, let the battles commence,
Till laughter erupts, as we tumble immense.

Hot chocolate dreams swirls in my cup,
While marshmallows perform a wiggle, then sup.
Chimneys are puffing with stories untold,
Of snowballs and slip-ups, shining like gold.

Jingle bells jingled, to a frosty old beat,
As one carol-er lost their frostbitten feet.
Underneath all the snow, mischief does dwell,
Crooning with giggles, winter's own spell.

Silent Etudes Beneath the Snow

Quiet the world, as the flakes do their dance,
While squirrels in mittens plot their next chance.
Frogs hidden away, under blankets of white,
Working on melodies of frosty moonlight.

Chilly chortles emerge from the trees,
As owls wear top hats, and dance in the breeze.
The wind plays a tune, off-key and so bold,
While melting drops giggle, as stories unfold.

Under the surface, where frost gently lays,
Fish toss snowballs, in rippling bays.
Nature's a jester, a whimsical sight,
With ice as confetti, painting the night.

While snowmen audition for Broadway's next show,
With carrots for cues, they steal the frosty glow.
A soft serenade from a winter's old heart,
Where silence can whisper, yet laughs play their part.

Frosty Visions and Vocal Verses

Beware of the shadow that quacks like a duck,
It's just an old snowman, with questionable luck.
Sirens in the snow, oh how they do wail,
Floating on sleds like a ship's merry sail.

Snowflakes argue about who's first to land,
A contest of patience, uncoordinated band.
With snowball precision, let the battles commence,
Till laughter erupts, as we tumble immense.

Hot chocolate dreams swirls in my cup,
While marshmallows perform a wiggle, then sup.
Chimneys are puffing with stories untold,
Of snowballs and slip-ups, shining like gold.

Jingle bells jingled, to a frosty old beat,
As one carol-er lost their frostbitten feet.
Underneath all the snow, mischief does dwell,
Crooning with giggles, winter's own spell.

Elegy of the Snowbound Spirit

In a blanket of white, I slipped with a grin,
A frosty surprise as I fell on my chin.
The snowflakes giggled, as they swirled all around,
While my winter wardrobe kept dragging me down.

The trees wore their coats, all sparkly and bright,
Their branches a chorus in the pale evening light.
With every soft crunch beneath clumsy feet,
Even icicles chuckled at my frosty defeat.

A snowman declared he'd be king of the hill,
Until a wild snowball left him mostly quite still.
We laughed with the wind, as it danced through the pines,

While the chill tickled noses with playful designs.

So here's to the folly this season bestows,
To the slapstick of winter, adorned with a pose.
With snowflakes a-twirling and spirits so bright,
Let's toast to the laughter that glimmers in white.

Pantomime of the Winter Woods

In the forest so still, where the shadows reside,
The squirrels put on shows, with acorns as their guide.
The snowdrifts applauded, with muffled delight,
As bunnies took stage, in their best costumes tight.

The trees whispered secrets, while giggling aloud,
As the brook that was frozen wore a glittery shroud.
~~The owls~~ in their wisdom shared jokes in the dark,
While the critters all gathered for the park's grand remark.

With a tap of my toe, I joined in the play,
Slipping on ice, in a most comical way.
The laughter was contagious, echoing through,
As even the sparrows hopped in for a cue.

So here's to the laughter, in winter's embrace,
Where nature's own humor finds its perfect place.
Each flake that falls softly, a tickle impart,
In this woodland extravaganza, we're all set to start.

Echoing Footsteps in the Ice

Crunch, crunch, the sound of my boots on the ice,
I twirl like a dancer, I feel very nice.
But oh, what a sight, as I slip on my rear,
The echoes just laugh, as I chuckle in cheer.

Shimmering crystals reflect my surprise,
While I dream of the summer, with warm sunny skies.
Yet who needs the heat when the cold brings such fun?
In this slapstick ballet, we glide, jump, and run!

I'll pretend I'm a penguin, waddling so bold,
With a snowball on standby, my aim's getting old.
The ice crackles softly, singing a tune,
While the sky laughs in colors beneath the full moon.

So let's join this dance, let our spirits take flight,
Every slip is a giggle worth savouring tonight.
With memories crafted through laughter and grace,
The season's playful antics bring joy to this place.

The Quiet Choir of the Cold

In the crisp morning air, the stillness does sway,
A choir of snowflakes begins their display.
With each soft little flurry, a tune fills the air,
As winter's own chorus sings lighthearted beware!

The rabbits in scarves hum a sweet frosty song,
As their ears flop about; oh, what could go wrong?
The pine trees join in, with a rustle and shake,
Dancing to rhythms they brew by the lake.

Icicles clink softly, like bells on a spree,
While the wind plays the harp as it wanders free.
A grand symphony echoes, with laughter in tow,
As snow people sway, putting on quite a show!

So come join the fun, let your spirit take flight,
Amidst this grand concert, we celebrate light.
Through the frosty still nights, where humor will lend,
A whimsical winter, where laughter's our friend.

Serenade of Frost and Silence

Whispers of snowflakes dance and twirl,
As penguins in tuxedos give a whirl.
Frosty breezes tickle the trees,
While squirrels wear scarves with the utmost ease.

A bunny with boots hops on the trail,
Chasing snowflakes as they set sail.
Icicles hang like chandeliers bright,
As the sun gives the frost a gentle bite.

Laughter rings out as skates glide by,
On frozen ponds where the snow ducks fly.
Snowmen with noses made of bright coal,
Wave at the kids, they're on a roll!

Yet beneath all this, the earth sneezes loud,
Warning the snowflakes, "Don't play in a crowd!"
With each little giggle, the cold takes a bow,
In the land of frost, fun is allowed!

Harmony of the Still White World

A snowball fight where no one can lose,
With slippery slides and wintery snooze.
In cozy igloos, we plot and we scheme,
While marshmallows dance in hot cocoa dream.

Crazy snow angels stretch out on the ground,
While the wind whistles tunes that are silly, profound.
A frosty old snowman cuddles a cat,
As penguins march home wearing woolly a hat.

Chilling chimes of ice hang from trees,
Alongside laughter and winter's sweet tease.
Even the owls wear bright little hats,
Gossiping softly with the friendly bats.

A dance of the frost, a jig in the air,
Rainbow snowflakes float without a care.
Echoes of chuckles in the icy stillness,
Give winter memories a giggly finesse!

Lullabies Underneath the Ice

Sleepy snow drifts wrap the world in a quilt,
As polar bears snore with a snuggly guilt.
The moonlight winks at the slumbering ground,
While icicles hum with a jingly sound.

Whispers of winter on a soft chilly night,
As owls serenade in soft and bright light.
A skater spins round, corkscrew and twirl,
Chasing snowflakes with a twinkling swirl.

Under the ice on the rivers below,
The fish tell stories while currents flow.
A crab wearing earmuffs, so snug and neat,
Joins the lullabies that keep time with the beat.

In cozy burrows, the critters snore on,
While the frost paints the picture until the dawn.
With each gentle chuckle, the night softly sighs,
As moonbeams embrace all the dreams in the skies!

Songs of the Shivering Ground

A chorus of chirps fills the frosty air,
With penguins in tuxes who strut with flair.
Hilarious antics as snowmen debate,
Who wears the best hat? Oh, it's quite a fate!

There's waltzing in snow, quite the funny sight,
As foxes in boots prance with all of their might.
The trees wear white gowns, all frosted and keen,
While mountains in laughter loom tall and serene.

The ground hums a tune, though it's chilly and blue,
With echoes of giggles in each snowy hue.
A blender-blade wind howls an odd little song,
Join the cold chorus, you can't go wrong!

As winter's cheeky breeze skips over the vale,
It's a jolly affair with each gust a tale.
So stomp on the ground with a chuckle and glee,
For laughter in frost is the key to be free!

Lullaby of Ice-Capped Peaks

The snowmen dance in quirky hats,
With frozen feet and furry cats.
They sing a tune, a silly cheer,
While igloos hum a song that's clear.

The penguins waddle, slip and slide,
In icy shoes, their joyful ride.
A polar bear with shades so bright,
Sips cocoa, basking in the light.

The mountains chuckle, iceflake's tease,
As chilly breezes dance with ease.
A snowball fight erupts with glee,
Who knew frost could be so free?

Oh, winter's whimsy, bright and bold,
With laughter wrapped in blankets cold.
A frosty giggle fills the air,
As snowflakes twirl without a care.

Twilight's Frosted Harmony

The icicles jingle, what a sound!
As snowflakes tumble to the ground.
A snow goose sings a frosty tune,
While polar lights perform at noon.

The squirrels wear their winter coats,
And waddle like the funniest goats.
In twilight's glow, they plan a feast,
With winter's treats, they're quite the beast!

The owls hoot jokes from trees so tall,
While frosty vines begin to sprawl.
A marzipan moon joins in the fun,
In this chilly playground, second to none.

Oh, let the breezes bring a smile,
In frosted night, we'll dance awhile.
The harmony of winter plays,
With silly hearts in snowy ways.

Reverberations in the Snow

The snowflakes tumble, giggling fast,
In pathways soft, they form a cast.
The rabbits hop, their ears on high,
As frosty whispers flit nearby.

A squirrel slips and spins to fall,
While laughing trees give nature's call.
The frozen brook plays hide and seek,
With glistening jokes and silly squeaks.

The echoes bounce off snowy walls,
As winter's humor gently calls.
A snowdrift shaped like a silly face,
Brings giggles to this winter place.

Oh, let the whispers of ice create,
A symphony that's truly great.
In this winter wonderland's tune,
We're all just children, under the moon.

Chorus of the Winter Stars

The stars twinkle in skies so bright,
As frosty gnomes break into flight.
They ride on sleds made of good cheer,
Singing songs for all to hear.

The moonlight drapes a shimmering scarf,
While snowflakes giggle, full of charm.
A chorus rises, crisp and clear,
In winter's grasp, we shed our fear.

The frosty winds join in the show,
Tickling noses as they blow.
A cosmic party, clumsy and fun,
In the wintry night, we've all just begun.

So let each star do a silly dance,
As we engage in winter's romance.
With laughter echoing up so far,
We're all a part of the winter star.

The Stillness Speaks

In winter's grip, the snowflakes play,
Wearing coats of white, they dance away.
They gather round, like friends at night,
With frosty jokes that spark delight.

The trees stand still, their branches bare,
But whisper secrets through the air.
They giggle softly, then shiver loud,
As squirrels scamper, feeling proud.

The chill does nothing to cool the jest,
As nature's humor puts us to the test.
Ice crystals laugh, a shimmering sight,
While penguins wobble, what a fright!

So let us chuckle with breath so white,
And revel in this frosty night.
For even stillness has tales to tell,
In the quirky world where cold things dwell.

Frosted Echoes of Distant Lands

In far-off lands where cold winds blow,
The penguins debate on which way to go.
They waddle along, unsure but spry,
As frosty echoes of giggles float by.

Icebergs grin with a frosty face,
As seals slide on like they're in a race.
"Catch me if you can!" they cry with glee,
While seals and snowflakes tumble free.

The arctic foxes play hide and seek,
In coats of white, so clever, so sleek.
They leap and chirp, a comical sight,
Making snowballs for a wild pillow fight!

So in this land of chill and cheer,
The frosted echoes ring loud and clear.
Laughter travels on the crisp, cold breeze,
Creating warmth in the heart with ease.

Chants of the Crystal Dawn

As dawn breaks pink on the frozen ground,
The ice crystals chime, what a joyful sound!
They jingle and jangle in morning's light,
While rabbits hop in a whimsical flight.

Chirps of the birds join in the fun,
Singing to the day, a new one begun.
They chirp in tunes both high and low,
Making the chill seem less like woe.

The frost-nipped leaves sway in delight,
Caught in a jig, oh what a sight!
With each dance step, the ground will laugh,
In nature's comedy, we find our path.

So raise a toast to the sparkling morn,
Where laughter and chill are happily worn.
For in every tune, every joyous sound,
Is a magic that lives in the frosty ground.

Songs of the Shivering Woods

In the woods so still, where shadows play,
The trees do chatter in their own way.
"Who's got the cold?" they tease and bark,
While critters scamper and leave their mark.

A squirrel slips and catches a branch,
With a squeal of laughter, what a chance!
"Oh, frosty friend, please lend a paw,
For tangled I am, in this icy draw!"

The owls hoot soft, in fits of mirth,
Cracking jokes about the frozen earth.
They sway and bob, in this winter tune,
Underneath the glow of a silvery moon.

So come join the fun in the shivering trees,
Where humor's as sweet as a cold-cropped breeze.
Let's all make merry, in the chill we find,
For laughter, like snowflakes, is beautifully kind.

Notes of a Glacial Heart

In the depths of ice, a heart may play,
With frozen beats, it waltzes away.
Snowmen gather, shake their heads,
As snowflakes dance upon their beds.

Penguins slide with silly grace,
Waddling through a wintry race.
Ice cubes chatter, clink, and cheer,
In frosty tunes, they spread good cheer.

Chill vibes only, the snowflakes say,
'Let's ice this party, hip-hip-hooray!'
In glacial kitchens, cupcakes rise,
Underneath these frost-kissed skies.

So grab your mittens, join the fun,
With frosty friends, the day's not done.
Laughter echoes through the freeze,
As winter whispers jokes with ease.

Serenade of the Still Woods

The trees are dressed in icy coats,
While squirrels wear their fluffy moats.
A woodpecker pecks to a frozen beat,
Knocking rhythms on frosty feet.

The brook, once bubbling, now hums low,
Giggling softly, it's put on a show.
A frozen frog croaks a dreadful tune,
In the stillness, he hopes to boon.

The owls hoot in a comical chat,
While bears scowl at this cold habitat.
Cheers grow louder, who needs a band?
When nature's humor is oh so grand!

Icicles hang with a glint of sass,
As winter invites all to come and pass.
Leaves all chuckle, they've lost their hue,
With jokes on the wind, the woods feel new.

The Solstice's Frozen Whisper

A snowman's grin stretches ear to ear,
Sending frosty giggles far and near.
Icicles jangle like bells of mirth,
Casting spells of joy on this frozen earth.

The nights grow long, but spirits stay bright,
As shadows dance under the pale moonlight.
Polar bears join in a clumsy twirl,
Feeling fabulous in a winter swirl.

Frosty friends in a chilly debate,
Who can slide best on this icy plate?
Snowflakes laugh as they tumble down,
Covering everything, kings of the crown.

Even the wind seems to chuckle and tease,
Blowing snowflakes like confetti in the breeze.
So let's raise a toast to this frozen cheer,
In winter's wonder, we hold so dear.

Winter's Silent Soliloquy

In silence wrapped like a cozy shawl,
Snow whispers secrets, a soft-spoken call.
Every flake tells tales of the past,
Of jolly snowballs and winters fast.

A snow rabbit hops with a flair so grand,
While owls doze off, dreaming of sand.
The frost fog rolls, thick as a plot,
And squirrels debate what to eat on the spot.

The trees stand guard with their icy tattoos,
Sharing old stories with the chilly blues.
Nobody listens, but giggles ensue,
As they all know winter's fun is true.

So come all ye merry, to the frost-kissed fields,
Where laughter and play are the greatest shields.
For amidst the stillness, joy will unfold,
In the heart of winter, let stories be told.